Newton's Wildlife Adventures
A Load of Rubbish

Written by
Yvonne Mcginlay

Concept and Illustrations
Simon Knott

Dedication
To all My Family and Friends For their Support and encouragement, Without WHoM this book Would Not Have been achieved.

Published in 2014 by Simon R Knott

Copyright © Yvonne Mcginlay 2014

Copyright © Simon Knott 2014

First Edition

The author asserts the moral right under the Copyright, Designs and Patents Act 1988 to be identified as the author of this work.

THiS BOOK BELONgS to

A Load of Rubbish

Arthur Tackle, a keen fisherman, was preparing for a fishing trip down by the Old Mill Pond where, legend has it, the biggest carp lurks beneath the waters. At least, that is what the local villagers believed, but over the years the story had become somewhat exaggerated.

Arthur was always telling the locals about his catches and his tales were a little elaborate to say the least, but this time he really did want to be the one to catch the biggest fish – the one that could never be caught, he thought to himself. What could be more glorious than that?

He had packed everything that would be required for his trip: his tent, fishing gear, bait, and all the food and drink he would need for the weekend.

After a good night's sleep full of dreams of his coming glory, Arthur woke, got dressed, brushed his teeth, put his camping equipment into his car and headed off to claim the trophy.

Along the winding country roads he drove, humming away to himself, ♪da dee dee dum da dee dee dum♪, but all he could think about was the prize at hand.

After about an hour he came to the Old Mill Pond. In the background stood Old Mill Farm, and this was the perfect spot to set up his tent. Time to get ready for some serious fishing!

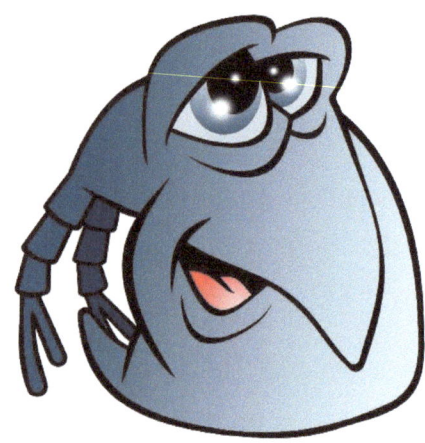

Out came the tent, which he put up quickly, hammering in the pegs to make sure everything was secure. Out came the fishing chair. Arthur put on his hat and waders with just enough time for a bit of lunch before he set up for a day's fishing – ham sandwiches with mustard, half a Scotch egg and a bottle of fizzy pop. PERFECT!

Arthur set out his chair, baited the end of his line and waited patiently until the sun set.

'Time for bed,' he said to himself, confident that tomorrow would bring him more luck. Arthur went to sleep and was soon snoring away.

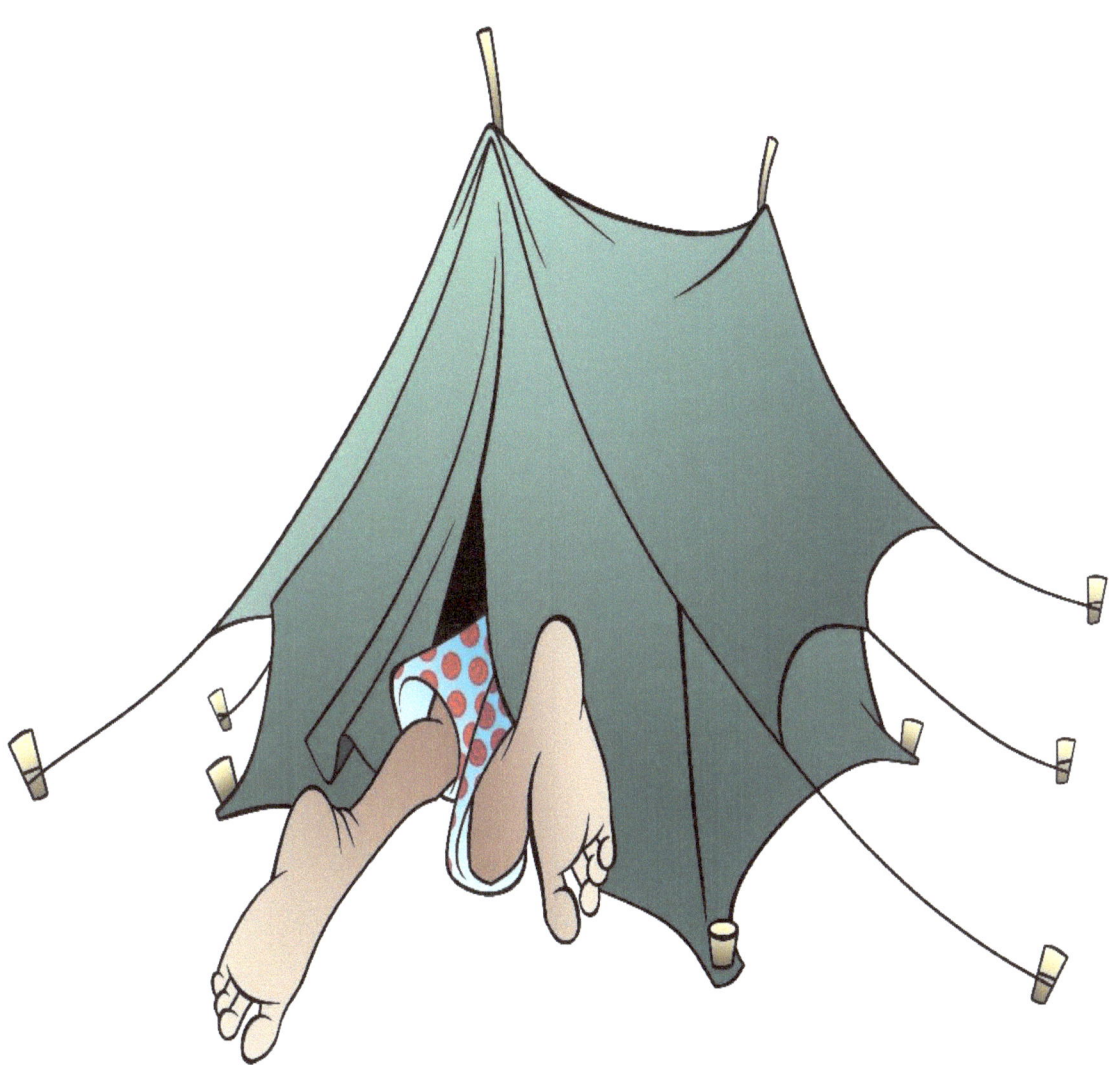

Beneath the waters, Newton the newt and his friends were aware of the fisherman above.

These friends included Karpa the carp, Perca the perch, Anod the swan mussel, Austo the crayfish, Blod the mosquito and Swift the dragonfly, who was always flitting around keeping an eye on everything going on around the old mill.

Swift informed Newton that the fisherman had just gone to bed for the night but that he looked set for a whole day's fishing the next day, so he was warning everyone to keep a lookout.

Karpa and Perca had already had a few near misses and they were determined not to get caught. 'Be careful, Karpa,' said Perca. 'You know you like showing off!'

Karpa laughed. 'I don't intend to get caught, but we need to be on the lookout. 'Everyone was restless and there was a lot of talk throughout the night.

Morning finally came and Arthur woke, stepped out of his sleeping bag and got dressed. He stretched and with a big yawn prepared breakfast: he lit his stove and cooked bacon and eggs before sitting down for a day's fishing. All was calm, and the friends, believing they had nothing to worry about, went about their business.

After several hours Arthur re-baited his line and cast out to the centre of the water. Karpa was swimming in the middle of the pond, showing off, at the very moment when the baited hook came crashing down into the water. The juicy lure of bread and sweetcorn looked so enticing to Karpa that he forgot for a moment that it was a trap and greedily swallowed the bait.

The whole pond went into major panic.

'Nooooo, Karpa!' yelled Newton. 'What are we going to do?' he cried. Arthur was excited: he had finally caught the great carp everyone had told him about. He reeled in the line until the fish was near his net, but Karpa suddenly managed to regain enough strength to swim back to the centre of the pond and dive under. With quick thinking Austo the crayfish swam over, cut the line and took the hook out, bringing Karpa to safety. Everyone was most concerned and made sure he was OK.

Arthur was so angry at losing his catch that he kicked his chair into the water, and, unbeknown to the friends, it floated to the bottom of the pond and trapped Anod the swan mussel.

Arthur was enraged and, muttering to himself, he packed everything into his car and drove off, leaving a whole mess behind: half-eaten sandwiches, burgers and Scotch eggs, plastic bottles, cans, packaging and bags. The mosquito decided to follow Arthur home and give him a little surprise of his own.

Poor Anod was unable to move but luckily the daphnia, who thought it was quite funny, had been floating around nearby and informed Newton that the mussel had been trapped, so he came over quickly.

The poor swan mussel could barely open his lid and could just about squeeze his arm out. Newton tried pulling as hard as he could. 'Oh, it's no good,' he thought to himself. He just could not move the chair, so he called over to Perca to come and help budge it.

Eventually Karpa and the crayfish helped too and together they managed to move the chair and free the swan mussel, who thanked his friends and was relieved to be free but was still his grumpy self.

Swift came over to see how everyone was and informed Newton that Blod was following the fisherman home, as he was planning a little surprise for him.

Newton said to everyone, 'We need to clear all this food up,' but Austo was already making short work of Arthur's leftovers.

'Look at greedy guts!' said Newton, as Austo stuffed his face with half a Scotch egg, chips, burgers and any other morsels he could see. 'I don't think we need to worry about clearing the food up.'

The wind had picked up quite a bit and some of the rubbish had blown into the pond. A banana skin on Perca's head was quite a sight to behold.

Newton suggested they bag up the plastic and other rubbish. 'Let's see how quickly we can work.'

Swift helped pick up everything that was left and Karpa and Perca swam around clearing the rubbish from the pond and putting it all in the big bag that Arthur had left behind.

They tied the top and in big red letters Newton painted on it: 'PLEASE RECYCLE'.

The friends decided that they must be very careful by the pond from now on, but just then Blod the mosquito returned with a smirk on his face. He had bitten Arthur Tackle on the nose and it had blown up like a big red balloon.

The friends had a good chuckle and were relieved that everyone was safe and the pond was back to normal.

AS NEWTON ALWAYS SAYS, BE CAREFUL AROUND PONDS AND RIVERS AND TAKE YOUR RUBBISH HOME WITH YOU.

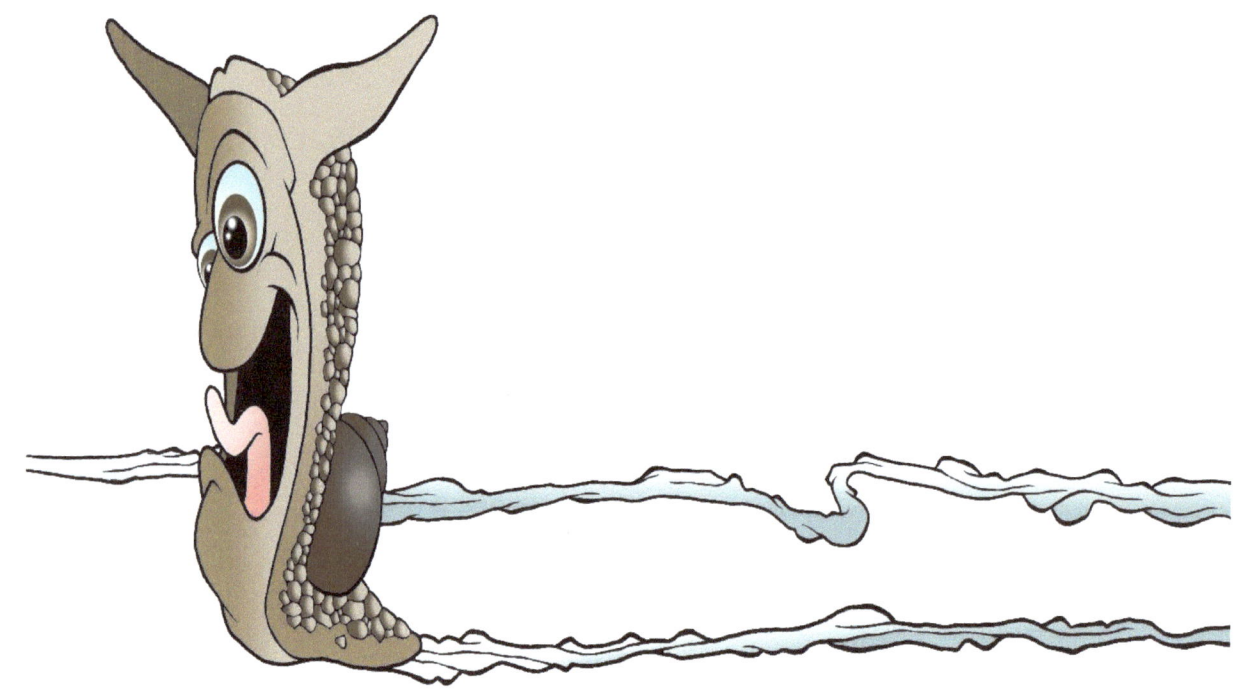

Newton's Fact File

Swan Mussel

Anodonta cygnea

An aquatic freshwater bivalve, native distribution from Europe to Siberian. The geographical distribution of this species is from the British Isles east to Siberia, and south into northern Africa. It can grow to 20 centimetres in length.

Common Carp

Cyprinus carpio

The common carp is a widespread freshwater fish of eutrophic (lake or pond) waters found in lakes and large rivers in Europe and Asia. It has been domesticated but wild populations are vulnerable to extinction.

European Perch

Perca fluviatilis

Commonly known as the European perch, red fin perch or English perch, this is a predatory species of fish found in Europe and Asia. It has five to nine dark vertical stripes and red pelvic, caudal and anal fins.

Southern Hawker (Dragonfly)

Aeshna cyanea

   The Southern or Blue Hawker is a 70-millimetre long species of hawker dragonfly. It is large, with a long body. It has green markings on its black body, and the males also has blue spots on the abdomen.

European Crayfish

Austropotamobius pallipes

   This is an endangered species of crayfish, native to Britain, and the only species of crayfish found in Ireland. It is commonly called the Atlantic stream or white-clawed crayfish and lives in canals, lakes, rivers and streams.

Mosquito

Anopheles claviger

   Common mosquitoes are also called 'house mosquitoes' because they are often seen in homes or near people. These mosquitoes are sometimes confused with winter gnats because gnats also form swarms and are attracted to lights on mild winter nights, just like common mosquitoes. Widely distributed throughout Britain, they breed in clean, brackish or dirty streams, ditches or ponds.

   Common mosquitoes are usually about six millimetres in length and have long thin bodies, which are a brown or grey colour. They also have two long antennae which are quite hairy and their wings are narrow and transparent.

New book coming soon:

Newton's Wildlife Adventures: Hydra and the Daphnianauts

Bonus drawings for you to colour in.

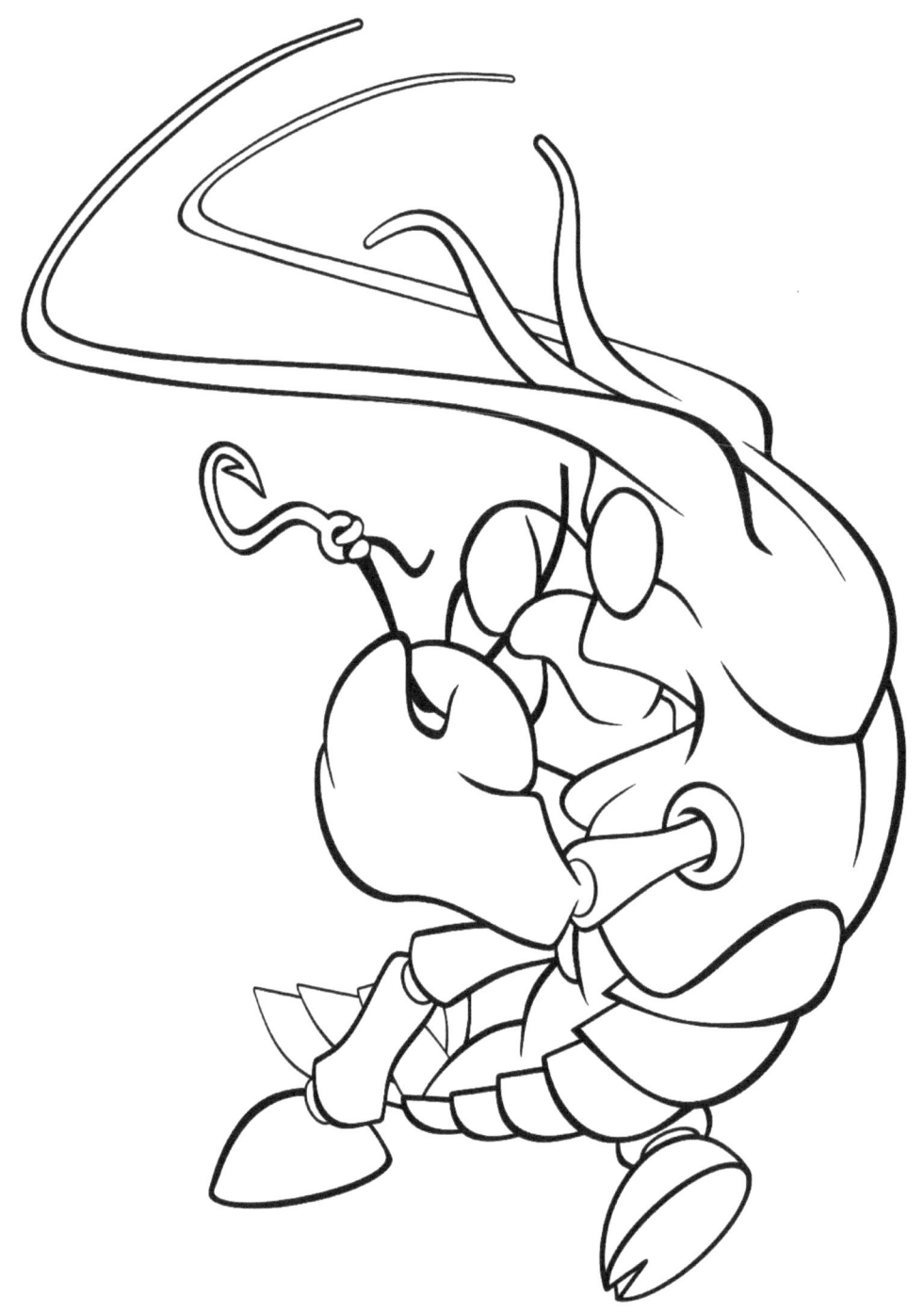

Simon Knott

Children's book illustrator, model maker and teacher

Studied illustration and holds a degree in model making from the well-respected UCA, Rochester, as well as a PGCE in higher education from Greenwich University.

Since this I have explored a wide range of different art mediums and have now developed a cartoon style utilising Photoshop on the computer. I love to put magic into children's books, covering science and nature with an environmental message.

www.simonrknott.com
siknotty@yahoo.co.uk

Yvonne Mcginlay

Children's book writer

I have been involved in Administration for the past 20 years, and have worked in many industries.

I am now working for SRK Illustrations and Cartoons as their sales, marketing and administrator and have now been given the opportunity to write the second book in the Newton Wildlife Adventures series.

From a young age I have always enjoyed writing, reading and telling stories, finding inspiration from nature.

ymcginlay@yahoo.co.uk